THE ALFRED BURT
CHRISTMAS CAROLS

Written in collaboration with
Bates G. Burt
Wihla Hutson

This anniversary edition is dedicated to Anne S. Burt
who devoted her life to sharing the Burt Carols with the world.

ISBN 978-0-634-09013-4

TRO ESSEX
MUSIC GROUP

EXCLUSIVELY DISTRIBUTED BY
HAL·LEONARD®

Visit Hal Leonard Online at
www.halleonard.com

www.alfredburtcarols.com

Contact us:
Hal Leonard
7777 West Bluemound Road
Milwaukee, WI 53213
Email: info@halleonard.com

In Europe, contact:
Hal Leonard Europe Limited
42 Wigmore Street
Marylebone, London, W1U 2RN
Email: info@halleonardeurope.com

In Australia, contact:
Hal Leonard Australia Pty. Ltd.
4 Lentara Court
Cheltenham, Victoria, 3192 Australia
Email: info@halleonard.com.au

INTRODUCTION

The Alfred Burt Carols originated in the small Upper Peninsula town of Marquette, Michigan. Alfred Burt was the son of the rector of St. Paul's Episcopal Church, Reverend Bates G. Burt, who started the Burt family tradition of sending an original carol as a Christmas card to friends and parishioners. Alfred joined his father and later Wihla Hutson in creating the series of Carols celebrated in this folio.

The Carols were first recorded in 1954 by the Columbia Choir and Brass Ensemble, were popularized by Fred Waring and his Pennsylvanians, and were licensed for print to Waring's Shawnee Press in three choral sets which are sung by choirs to this day. After Alfred Burt's untimely death that year, his wife Anne devoted her life to the care of the Carols and their daughter Diane, who now continues this legacy. With the help and support of Diane's husband and partner, Nick D'Amico, these American Christmas classics will continue to thrive for generations to come.

Over the years the Carols have been individually recorded by a wide range of artists from Nat King Cole to James Taylor. This 50th anniversary folio includes a current Burt Carols discography, a story of each Carol told in the words of Alfred's wife, Anne S. Burt, and a replication of the original Burt family Christmas card.

CONTENTS

CHRISTMAS COMETH CAROLING

Carol for 1942: This was the year that the father-son writing team began. Alfred Burt had just graduated from the University of Michigan as an outstanding student of music theory. He was a member of the marching band, The Little Symphony Orchestra, Phi Mu Alpha music fraternity, and played trumpet with the dance band at the Michigan Union. His musical abilities were nurtured by teachers who respected his new harmonies.

"Now that you are the professional musician, would you compose the music for the family card?" was Reverend Burt's invitation.

So while on a date with Al, I waited and talked with Reverend Burt. In fifteen minutes, Al wrote the setting for "O Christmas Cometh Caroling," a carol written by Father Andrew, a Catholic priest from England. His book of carols was purchased at a church bazaar by Reverend Burt.

(It was not included in the original publications, for I had to clear the copyright in England, finding that Father Andrew had died just a few years before.)

Christmas 1942

CHRISTMAS COMETH CAROLING

Words by
FATHER ANDREW

Music By
ALFRED BURT

Moderately slow (♩ = about 80)

| A | E | A7 | F#m |

1. Oh Christ-mas com-eth car-ol-ing, And
2. And it would be a shame to tell That
3. Then shrive you clean and wash you white. Keep

| Bm7 | C#m | D | C#7sus C#7 | F#m | C#m | Bm7 | C#m |

all the mer-ry bells do ring. To tell how an-gels once did sing,
on-ly clang of bra-zen bell Should play earth's part His praise to swell.
vi-gil well this ho-ly night. While an-gels car-ol in the height,

| Dm | Dm7 | Bbmaj7 | Bm6 | Am | Em | Asus | A |

Kneel-ing a-bout their Ba-by King, Born of our La-dy Ma-ry.
It must be you and I as well, Who kneel to La-dy Ma-ry.
We shall re-ceive ere dawn of light Bread from the Babe of Ma-ry.

JESU PARVULE
(Poor Little Jesus)

Words by
BATES G. BURT

Music by
ALFRED BURT

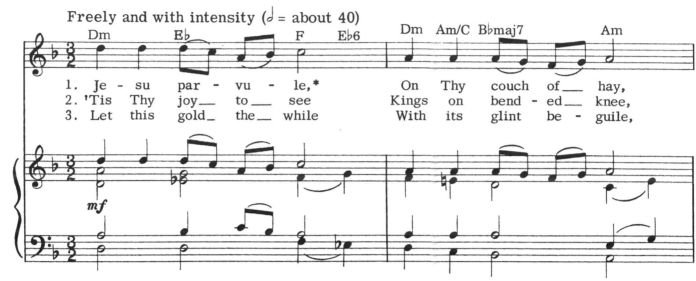

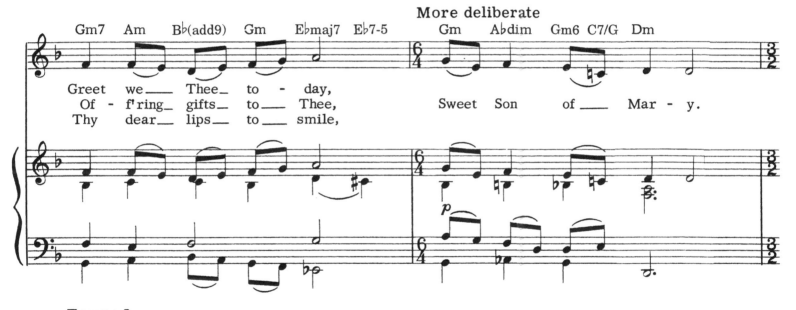

* Pronounced "Yay-soo par-voo-lay"

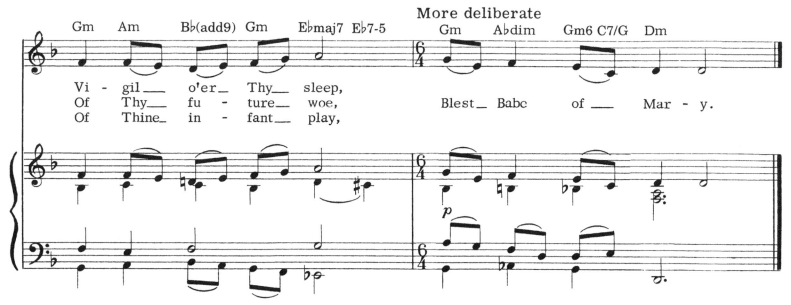

Vi - gil___ o'er___ Thy___ sleep,
Of Thy___ fu - ture___ woe,
Of Thine_ in - fant___ play,

Blest_ Babe of ___ Mar - y.

JESU PARVULE (Poor Little Jesus)

Carol for 1943: With World War II upon us, the lyrics for the next carols were mailed to Texas where Al was serving with the 616th Army Air Force Band. Many of his friends from the University of Michigan Band had also joined with him. He had agonized over his feelings of pacifism, but after much soul searching entered the service in a non-combatant role.

— CHRISTMAS GREETINGS —

JESU PARVULE,
ON THY COUCH OF HAY,
GREET WE THEE TODAY,
    SWEET SON OF MARY!
BE THY SLUMBER DEEP
WHILE FAIR ANGELS KEEP
VIGIL O'ER THY SLEEP.
    BLEST BABE OF MARY.

'TIS THY JOY TO SEE
KINGS ON BENDED KNEE
OFFERING GIFTS TO THEE,
    SWEET SON OF MARY.
BUT THOU MAY'ST NOT KNOW
WHAT THESE GIFTS FORESHOW
OF THY FUTURE WOE,
    BLEST BABE OF MARY.

LET THIS GOLD THE WHILE
WITH ITS GLINT BEGUILE
THY DEAR LIPS TO SMILE,
    SWEET SON OF MARY.
MAY NO SHADOW GRAY
CLOUD ONE HAPPY DAY
OF THINE INFANT PLAY
    BLEST BABE OF MARY.

REV. BATES G. BURT   SGT. ALFRED S. BURT
                            OCT. 10, 1943

Andante con moto

Je-su par-vu-le, On Thy couch of hay, Greet we Thee to-day,

Sweet Son of Ma-ry!   Be Thy slum-ber deep,

While fair an-gels keep   Vi-gil o'er Thy sleep, Blest Babe of Mary.

WHAT ARE THE SIGNS (Carol In War-Time)

Carol for 1944: Al continued his work in Texas, now a Staff Sergeant, fronting a concert band and a dance band called the "Yardbirds." He was an occasional substitute with the Houston Symphony Orchestra on trumpet. The dance band broadcast over the Texas airwaves. Al was arranging, as well as singing and playing. My contact with Al was slight during the war years, but this card opened the lines of communication again. A hurried visit while on leave led to our engagement.

WHAT ARE THE SIGNS

Words by
BATES G. BURT

Music by
ALFRED BURT

AH, BLEAK AND CHILL THE WINTRY WIND

Christmas 1945

Words by
BATES G. BURT

Music by
ALFRED BURT

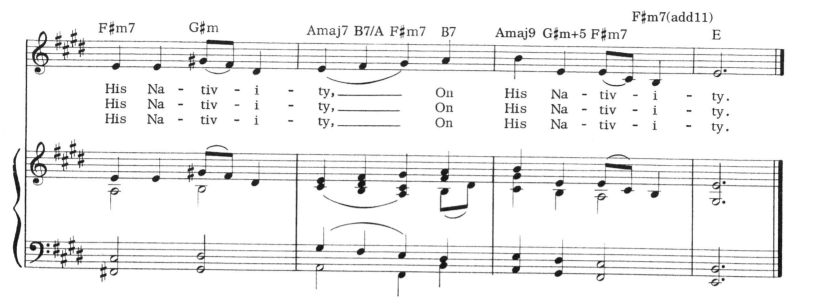

His Na - tiv - i - ty, _____ On His Na - tiv - i - ty.
His Na - tiv - i - ty, _____ On His Na - tiv - i - ty.
His Na - tiv - i - ty, _____ On His Na - tiv - i - ty.

Dark, dark the night when Christ was born,
But deeper shadows be
Within the heart that hath no joy
With Mary and her Heavenly Boy
On His Nativity.

Peace be to them and right good cheer
Who carol merrily,
And hie them forth when church bells ring
To kneel before their new-born King
On His Nativity

B.G.B.

AH, BLEAK AND CHILL
THE WINTRY WIND

Carol for 1945: A new name was added to the Burt family card...mine. As Al's sweetheart, I had been in the background of his life, sharing Young People's Society, the choir, school activities, and the "big bands" of the era. His sister, Deborah, had been my music teacher in high school and his father was my clergyman. I was in training to teach kindergarten through third grade at Michigan State Normal College. I sang at the League in Ann Arbor, but our college days were too full to see much of each other except on breaks at the church.

During the war I joined the Navy as a Wave and spent my war years at the U.S. Naval Hospital in San Diego, California. My days were filled with my duties as an operating room technician, and my nights were filled singing with the dance bands. Al and I were married in October, just before his mother, Emily May, died of cancer.

ALL ON A CHRISTMAS MORNING
(Oh, Who Are These That Throng The Way)

Words by
BATES G. BURT

Music by
ALFRED BURT

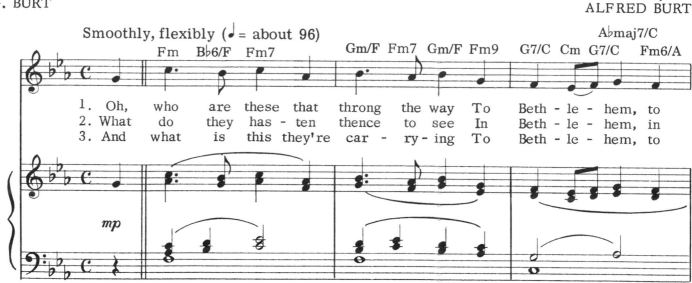

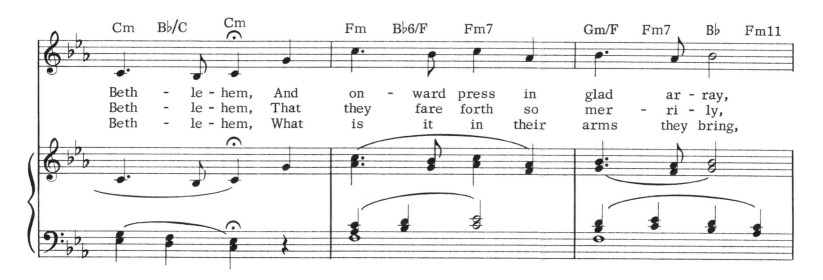

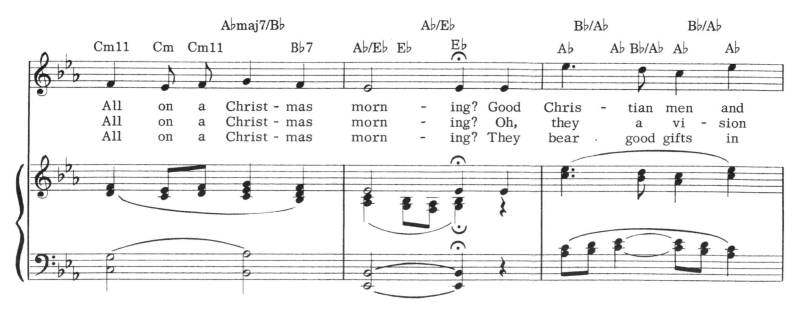

ALL ON A CHRISTMAS MORNING
(Oh, Who Are These That Throng The Way)

Carol for 1946: The one time we were together with Father Burt for a carol preview was for the 1946 carol. We had gone to "camp" in Marquette to visit him. We spent an evening at the home of "Aunt" Grace Spaulding, an art instructor. Al had written the music early and shared it on that summer evening. How Dad Burt's eyes sparkled as he heard his words come to life in the melody. He had Al play it over and over singing along. It was a special moment, and it is a warm memory I have of these two men who respected each other in the music they shared.

2. What do they hasten thence to see
   In Bethlehem, in Bethlehem,
   That they fare forth so merrily,
   All on a Christmas morning?
   Oh, they a vision fair would view,
   Would find the beautiful and true,
   And faith and hope and love renew,
   All on a Christmas morning.

3. And what is this they're carrying
   To Bethlehem, to Bethlehem?
   What is it in their arms they bring,
   All on a Christmas morning?
   They bear good gifts in rich excess
   Of love and joy and thankfulness,
   With which mankind they fain would bless,
   All on a Christmas morning. —1946

NIGH BETHLEHEM (Nigh Beth'lem On A Wintry Night)

Carol for 1947: This was the last carol Al and his father wrote together. Dad Burt died the following year while in relief at a parish outside Towson, Maryland where his daughter Deb and her husband Bill were living. Al and I were in New York City where he taught sight singing at the American Theater Wing School and played casuals in local bands. It was our last Christmas with Dad. The carol "Nigh Bethlehem" is a musical story of Christ's birth. Not all the verses were used in choral publications. Here you find all of them. The first Burt carols are influenced by the church, so much a part of the Bates G. Burt heritage.

Bates G. Burt.   Alfred S. Burt.

1. Nigh Beth-le'm on a win-try night (No-ël! no-ël! no-ël!), Poor shep-herds saw a love-ly sight, When an-gel hosts in ves-ture bright Burst forth from heav-ens loft-ty height, And sang "No-ël! no-ël——!" And sang "No-ël! no-ël——!"

2. Then did these shepherds upward gaze,
(Noël! Noël! Noël!)
And harked to voices singing praise
In merry and melodious lays
To One they called "Ancient of Days,
And sang "Noël! Noël!"

3. "Be not afraid!" an angel cries;
(Noël! Noël! Noël!)
"We bring you tidings from the skies;
"The Christ is born! Shepherds, arise!
"Go seek the manger where He lies,
"And sing 'Noël! Noël!'"

4. Swift sped the herdsmen on their way
(Noël! Noël! Noël!)
To Bethlehem ere break of day;
And there in swaths upon the hay
The Holy Child of Mary lay.
(Come sing Noël! Noël!)

5. Three wise men came from lands afar,
(Noël! Noël! Noël!)
From Persia, Ind and Zanzibar,
Led onward by a mystic star,-
Melchior, Gaspar, Bel-thazar.
(Come sing Noël! Noël!)

6. Peace and Good Will the Christ Child brings,
(Noël! Noël! Noël!)
And saves all men from evil things;
For He of Whom the angel sings
Is Lord of Lords and Kings;
(Then sing Noël! Noël!)

7. So, Christian folk, put fear aside,
(Noël! Noël! Noël!)
And spread the Gospel far and wide,
That joy be great at Christmastide,
And God in Christ be magnified.
(Then sing Noël! Noël!)

NIGH BETHLEHEM
(Nigh Beth'lem On A Wintry Night)

Words by
BATES G. BURT

Music by
ALFRED BURT

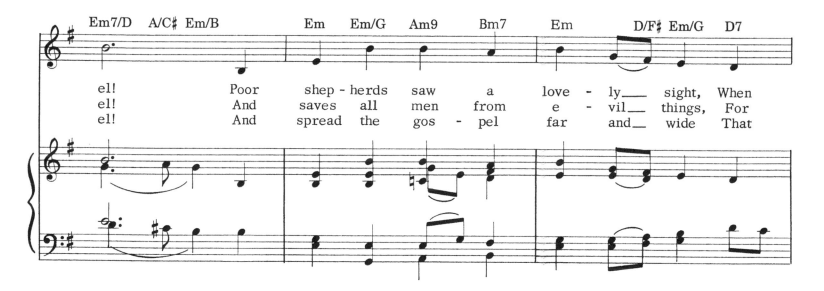

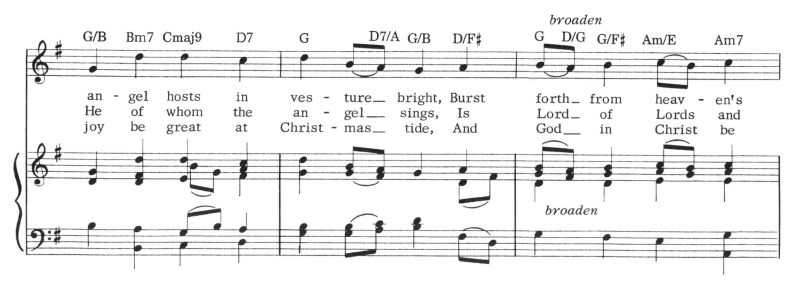

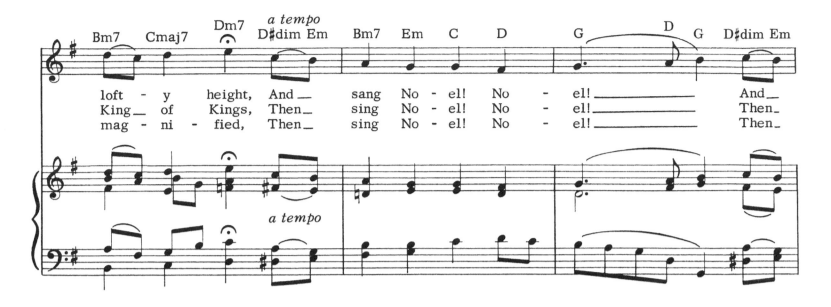

These verses are in the order of the original Christmas card. For a shorter version of this carol, we suggest the verses under the music.

Nigh Bethle'm on a wintry night,
Noel! Noel! Noel!
Poor shepherds saw a lovely sight
When angel hosts in vesture bright
Burst forth from heaven's lofty height,
And sang "Noel! Noel!"

Then did these shepherds upward gaze,
Noel! Noel! Noel!
And harked to voices singing praise
In merry and melodious lays
To One they called "Ancient of Days,"
And sang "Noel! Noel!"

"Be not afraid!" an angel cries.
Noel! Noel! Noel!
"We bring you tidings from the skies;
"The Christ is born! Shepherds, arise!
"Go seek the manger where He lies,
"And sing 'Noel! Noel!' "

Swift sped the herdsmen on their way,
Noel! Noel! Noel!
To Bethlehem ere break of day;
And there in swaths upon the hay,
The Holy Child of Mary lay.
Come sing "Noel! Noel!"

Three wise men came from lands afar,
Noel! Noel! Noel!
From Persia, Ind and Zanzibar,
Led onward by a mystic star,
Melchior, Gaspar, Balthazar.
Come sing "Noel! Noel!"

Peace and goodwill the Christ Child brings,
Noel! Noel! Noel!
And saves all men from evil things,
For He of whom the angel sings
Is Lord of Lords and King of Kings,
Then sing "Noel! Noel!"

So, Christian folk, put fear aside,
Noel! Noel! Noel!
And spread the gospel far and wide
That joy be great at Christmastide,
And God in Christ be magnified,
Then sing "Noel! Noel!"

CHRIST IN THE STRANGER'S GUISE

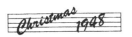

An old English rune of hospitality

Music by
ALFRED BURT

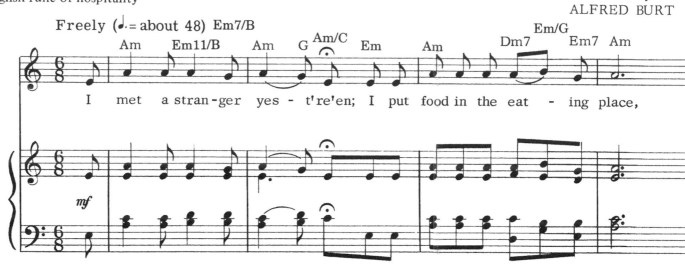

I met a stran-ger yes - t're'en; I put food in the eat - ing place,

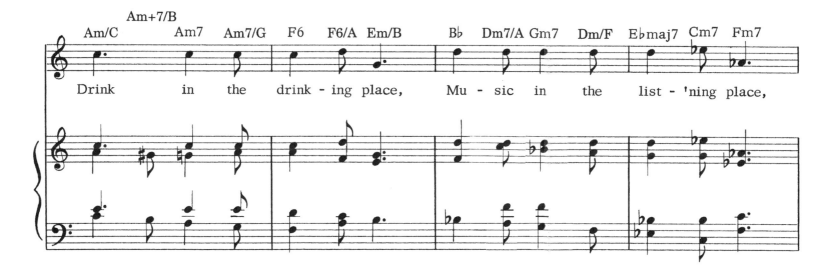

Drink in the drink-ing place, Mu - sic in the list - 'ning place,

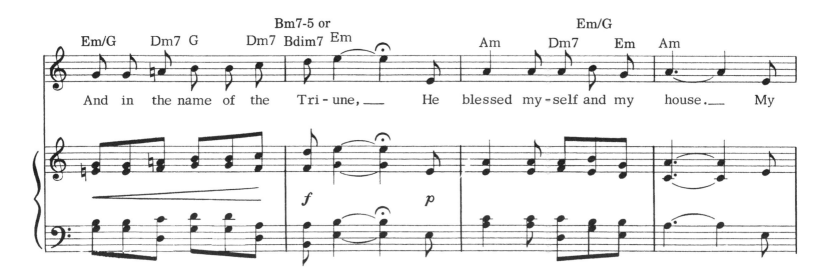

And in the name of the Tri - une, __ He blessed my-self and my house. __ My

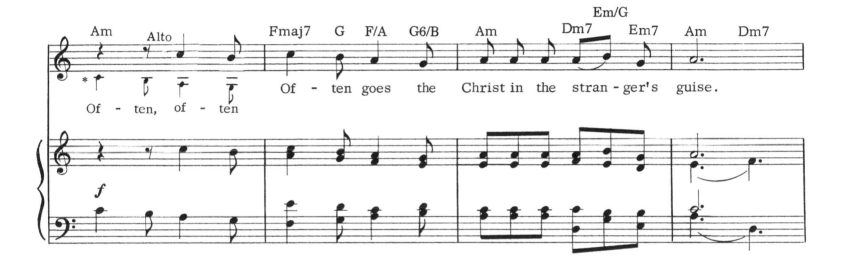

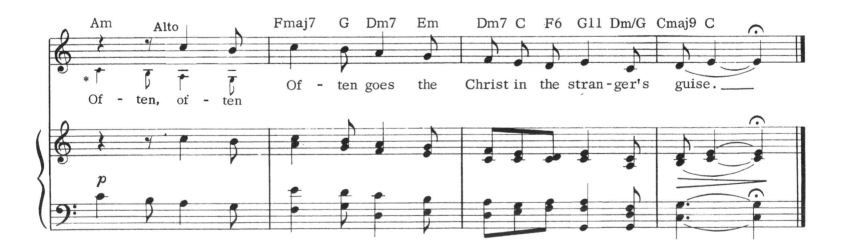

CHRIST IN THE STRANGER'S GUISE

Carol for 1948: Al and I decided it was our natural transition to carry on the tradition. So, on the train back to New York (after Dad Burt's funeral), we made the decision to continue the Christmas cards. With our lyricist gone, we were able to find lyrics for this carol thanks to John Burt, Al's brother. He had discovered an old English rune of hospitality on the wall of the Dean's study at Virginia Theological Seminary. His gift of the copy gave us the lovely "Christ in a Stranger's Guise," the original of which hangs over the family Steinway, a gift from Father Burt when he closed the Pontiac house. The English rune stands as a symbol of hospitality representing both generations of the Burts.

CAROL OF THE MOTHER (Sleep, Baby Mine)

Carol for 1949: Wihla Hutson, church organist at All Saints' Pontiac and long time family friend, had shared many Christmases with the Burts. It was the remembrance of her poetic talents for the traditional family stocking gifts that prompted us to ask her to take our ideas and put them into words. She accepted, as she had long admired Al's special gift of music.

These writings were as spontaneous and as much a part of our Christmas celebrations as our gifts, gatherings, or entertaining friends. We chose to express our joy in the gift of music. Wihla wrote the words from our ideas, Al set them to music, and I got the family card ready.

Expecting our first child, I was sent off to my family's home at Oxbow Lake outside Pontiac, Michigan. Al went on to California and another tour with the Alvino Rey Orchestra. We thought it best for me to stay confined until the baby arrived. I loved being back in familiar places, renewing old friendships, and returning to All Saints' where Wihla Hutson still gave her beautiful organ backgrounds to the choir.

It was on a night shared together that Wihla and I were conversing about our needs and wishes for the 1949 carol. I babbled about the new life inside me. Al and I had decided on a lullaby that would be sent as a birth announcement as well as a card. But it was my chatter about wanting a carol which spoke to the universality of Christ in the eyes of children that prompted the carol, "Some Children See Him." Our ideas were turned over to Wihla and she penned words for both carols at the same time.

Carol of the Mother

Sleep, baby mine!
A golden star is burning
In God's clear blue above,
And O! my heart is learning
The miracle of Love.

Sleep, baby mine!
I hear an angel singing
Above thy tiny bed;
The scent of Heav'n is clinging
About thy tiny head.

Sleep, baby mine!
To me, who humbly bore thee
Thy cradle is a throne,
But all the days before thee
Are known to God alone.

Anne and Al Burt

CAROL OF THE MOTHER
(Sleep, Baby Mine)

Christmas 1949

Words by
WIHLA HUTSON

Music by
ALFRED BURT

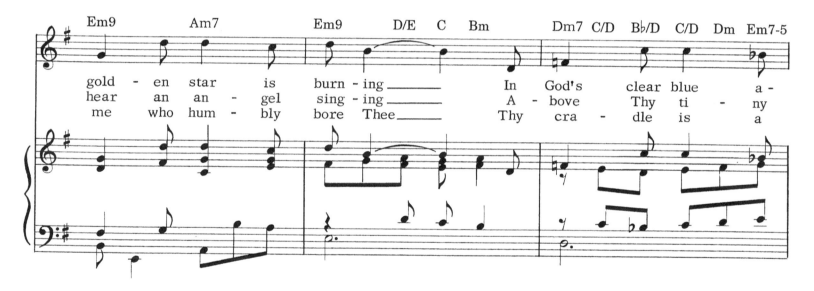

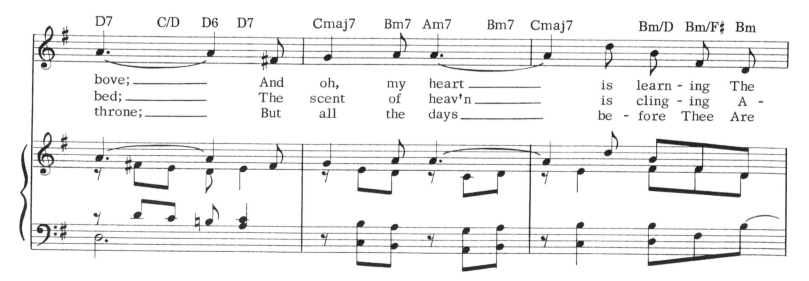

THIS IS CHRISTMAS (Bright, Bright The Holly Berries)

Carol for 1950: This year found us in California. Al had not returned for the birth of Diane Bates Burt on March 8, 1950. The very bad weather caused me to advise him that this was a job for Dr. Vernon Abbott and myself. But he kept in close touch while on the road and the night she was born, a very moving chorus of "Diane" on the trumpet announced her arrival to the band members. As soon as she could travel, we joined Al in Los Angeles. At the airport, he met for the first time the one person who would rival his devotion to music.

The carols now reflected the life-style of our young family. Al and I established a pattern of a secular then sacred setting for the family card. Wihla mailed the words to "Bright, Bright the Holly Berries," which express the secular joys of the season. (The sacred third verse in the songbook was added later.) Diane was only interested in the tinsel and wrapping paper that first Christmas.

THIS IS CHRISTMAS
(Bright, Bright The Holly Berries)

Words by
WIHLA HUTSON

Music by
ALFRED BURT

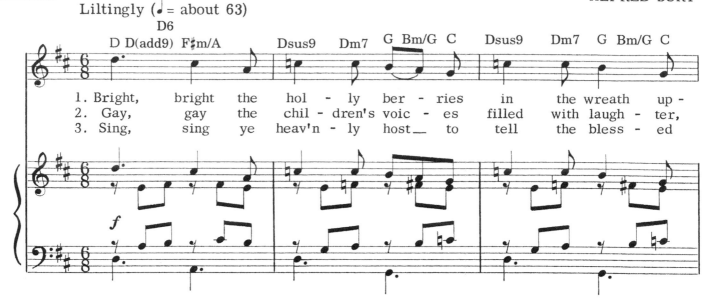

1. Bright, bright the hol-ly ber-ries in the wreath up-
2. Gay, gay the chil-dren's voic-es filled with laugh-ter,
3. Sing, sing ye heav'n-ly host__ to tell the bless-ed

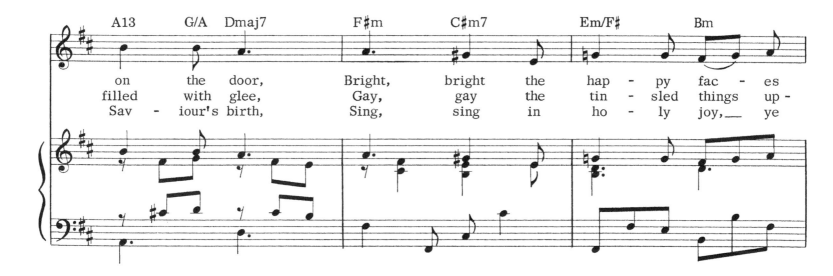

on the door, Bright, bright the hap-py fac-es
filled with glee, Gay, gay the tin-sled things up-
Sav-iour's birth, Sing, sing in ho-ly joy,__ ye

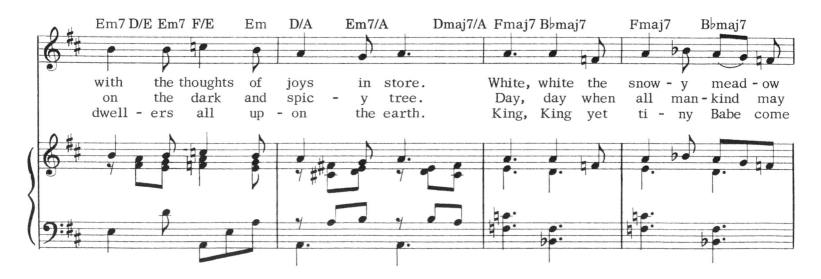

with the thoughts of joys in store. White, white the snow-y mead-ow
on the dark and spic-y tree. Day, day when all man-kind may
dwell-ers all up-on the earth. King, King yet ti-ny Babe come

SOME CHILDREN SEE HIM

Words by
WIHLA HUTSON

Music by
ALFRED BURT

Christmas 1951

Slowly (♩ = about 42)

Lyrics:

1. Some chil-dren see Him lil-y white, The Ba-by Je-sus born this night. Some chil-dren see Him lil-y white, With tress-es soft and fair. Some chil-dren see Him bronzed and brown, The Lord of heav'n to earth come down; Some

2. Some chil-dren see Him al-mond eyed, This Sav-iour whom we kneel be-side, Some chil-dren see Him al-mond eyed, With skin of yel-low hue. Some chil-dren see Him dark as they, Sweet Mar-y's Son to whom we pray; Some

3. The chil-dren in each dif-f'rent place Will see the Ba-by Je-sus' face Like theirs, but bright with heav'n-ly grace, And filled with ho-ly light. O lay a-side each earth-ly thing, And with thy heart as of-fer-ing, Come

chil - dren see Him bronzed and_ brown,   With   dark and heav - y_ hair.
chil - dren see Him dark as_ they,   And   ah! they love   him   too!
wor - ship now the In - fant_ King,   'Tis   love that's born   to - night!

SOME CHILDREN SEE HIM

Carol for 1951: Following the secular, then sacred pattern, "Some Children See Him" was sent in 1951, even though it was penned at the same time as the 1949 lullaby, "Sleep, Baby Mine." I was very grateful to hear, after one road trip with the baby, that we would stay in the San Fernando Valley. We were happy to be establishing roots in one place. We joined a church and Al became active in all phases of the Hollywood music world.

COME, DEAR CHILDREN

Words by
WIHLA HUTSON

Music by
ALFRED BURT

Lightly, jubilantly (♩. = about 84)

1. Come, dear chil-dren, don't be dal-ly-ing, All the fam-'ly now is ral-ly-ing, Not a mo-ment now to spare, Joy-ful haste is in the air. There are nuts to crack and
2. Now be-gins a might-y scur-ry-ing, Each to do his task is hur-ry-ing, All to fin-ish he con-trives, Ere the glo-rious day ar-rives. There are gifts to wrap and
3. Was there ev-er such a jol-ly day, Fam-'lies gath-er'd for the hol-i-day, Home is fill'd with danc-ing eyes, Laugh-ter, love and glad sur-prise. There are friends to see and

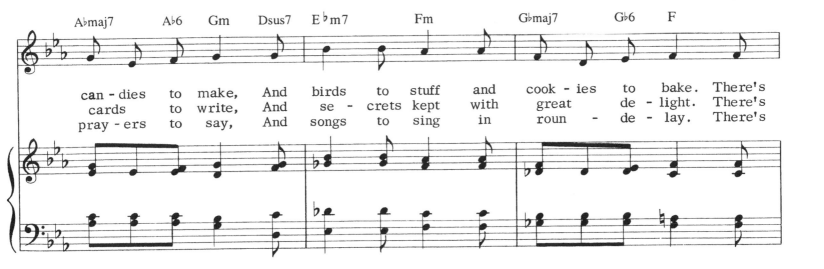
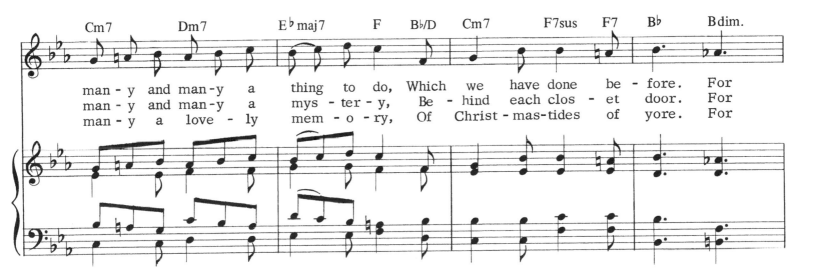
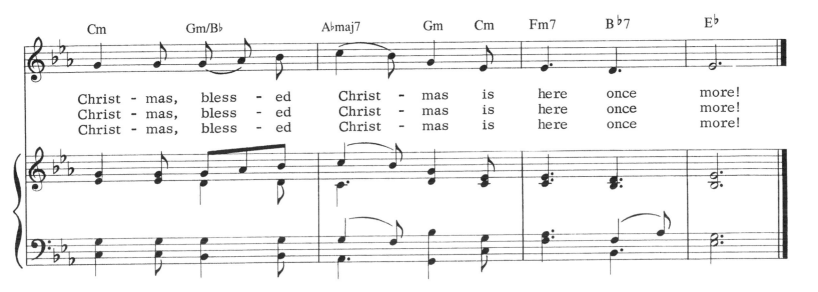

COME, DEAR CHILDREN

Carol for 1952: The carol was finished at the rehearsal of the Blue Reys, the singing group with Alvino Rey's Orchestra. Al asked them to sing it so that he could check the harmonies. They liked it so much that they asked Al if they could add it to their performance at the King Sisters' Christmas party. It was the hit of the party! This was the introduction of the carols to the Hollywood music crowd.

words by
Wihla Hutson

music by
Alfred Burt

Come, dear children, don't be dal-ly-ing All the fam-'ly now is ral-ly-ing; Not a mo-ment now to spare, Joy-ful haste is in the air. There are nuts to crack and candies to make, And birds to stuff and cookies to bake, There's ma-ny and ma-ny a thing to do, Which we have done be-fore, For Christmas, bless-ed Christ - mas is here once more!

Come, dear children, don't be dallying
All the family now is rallying,
Not a moment now to spare
Joyful haste is in the air.
There are nuts to crack
and candies to make,
And birds to stuff
and cookies to bake,
There's many and many a thing to do
Which we have done before,
For Christmas, blessed Christmas,
Is here once more!

Now begins a mighty scurrying;
Each to do his task is hurrying.
All to finish he contrives
Ere the glorious day arrives.
There are gifts to wrap
And cards to write,
And secrets kept
With great delight.
There's many and many a mystery
Behind each closet door,
For Christmas, blessed Christmas,
Is here once more!

Was there ever such a jolly day!
Families gathered for the holiday;
Home is filled with dancing eyes,
Laughter, love and glad suprise.
There are friends to see
And prayers to say,
And songs to sing
In roundelay
There's many a lovely memory
Of Christmastides of yore,
For Christmas, blessed Christmas,
Is here once more!

words by
Wihla Hutson   1952   music by
Alfred Burt

Anne, Al and Diane Burt

O HEARKEN YE

Carol for 1953: We had just moved into our first home and we were expecting another baby. But this expectation would not be fulfilled. We learned that Al had lung cancer, and I lost the baby. The prognosis gave Al six months to a year to live! But little time was spent on grief as the days were filled with doctors, hospital tests, a confirmation trip to the Memorial Hospital in New York City. My husband had not been very ill in any of his life. He did not like hospitals, and the fact that I could nurse him at home led us to change our lovely master bedroom into a hospital suite. We filled each day in a loving, serene atmosphere. Al's humor, warmth, compassion, and non-complaining disposition made each day a blessing. Ours was a happy, loving family despite the tribulations.

We chose this rousing, processional-like hymn as our final family card together. Al and I needed the inspiring words as much as those who shared our days against lung cancer. Al's faith and courage were undaunted. He was tired of the struggle, but he vowed to keep Diane's world happy. His gift of her childhood in his last year was an unselfish act he chose himself. Our family faced each day as it dawned with much support from family and friends. He played the accompaniment of the carols, both old and new, at the King family party that year, but he was confined to bed shorty after that.

A Merry Christmas

from

The Burts
Anne, Al, Diane

O hearken, ye who long for peace,   O hearken, ye who long for love,

Your troubled searching now may   And turn your hearts to God
                              cease;   above.

Gloria, Gloria, In excelsis Deo!   Gloria, Gloria, In excelsis Deo!

For at His cradle you shall find   The angels' song the wonder tells:

God's healing grace for all mankind.   Now Love Incarnate with us dwells!

Gloria, Gloria, In excelsis Deo!   Gloria, Gloria, In excelsis Deo!

O HEARKEN YE

Christmas 1953

Words by
WIHLA HUTSON

Music by
ALFRED BURT

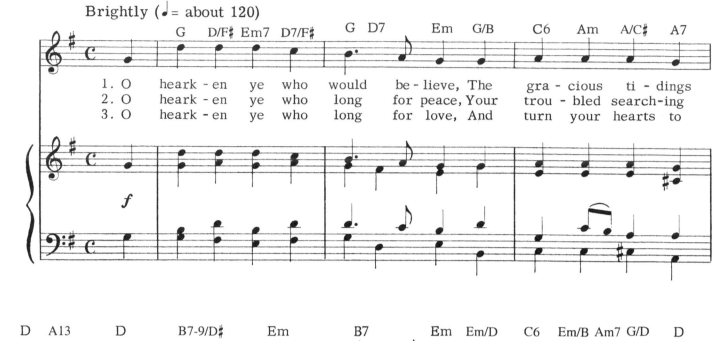

day is come to hu - man birth.
heal - ing grace for all man - kind.
Love In - car - nate with us dwells! Glo - ri - a,

glo - ri - a, In ex - cel - sis De - o.

Our friends in the music business alerted Jim Conkling, President of Columbia Records and brother-in-law to one of the King Sisters, of the urgency of Al's condition. He wanted to record the carols. It gave Al a goal those last few months. Wihla was asked to write new lyrics for the recording. She told me that all she needed was Al's request and the words flowed so fast she could hardly write them down. ("We'll Dress the House" and "Caroling, Caroling" were the result.)

WE'LL DRESS THE HOUSE

Words by
WIHLA HUTSON

Music by
ALFRED BURT

1. We'll dress this house with hol-ly bright And sprigs of mis-tle-toe; We'll trim the Christ-mas tree to-night And set the lights a-glow; We'll wrap our gifts with
2. We'll dress the ta-ble dain-ti-ly, Our fin-est treas-ures use, That all a-spar-kle it may be And bright with love-ly hues; Then for the feast-ing
3. And ye who would the Christ Child greet Your heart al-so a-dorn, That it may be a dwell-ing meet For Him who now is born. Let all un-love-ly

This carol was not sent as a Burt Christmas card.

CAROLING, CAROLING

Words by
WIHLA HUTSON

Music by
ALFRED BURT

This carol was not sent as a Burt Christmas card.

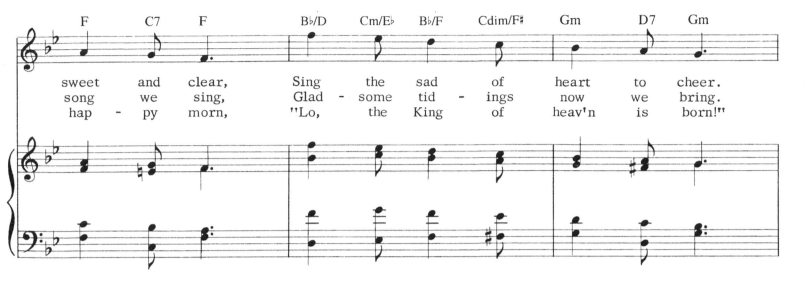

sweet   and   clear,   Sing   the   sad   of   heart   to   cheer.
song   we   sing,   Glad - some   tid - ings   now   we   bring.
hap - py   morn,   "Lo,   the   King   of   heav'n   is   born!"

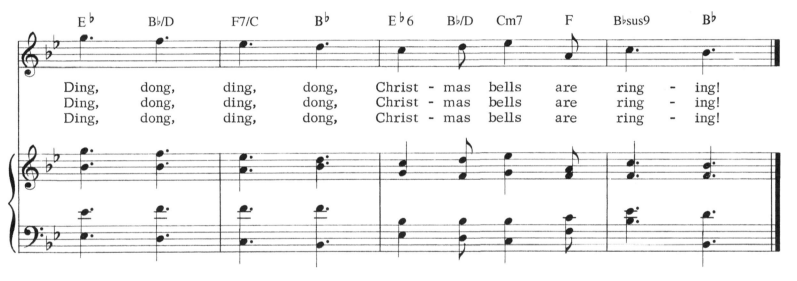

Ding,   dong,   ding,   dong,   Christ - mas   bells   are   ring - ing!
Ding,   dong,   ding,   dong,   Christ - mas   bells   are   ring - ing!
Ding,   dong,   ding,   dong,   Christ - mas   bells   are   ring - ing!

THE STAR CAROL

Christmas 1954

Words by
WIHLA HUTSON

Music by
ALFRED BURT

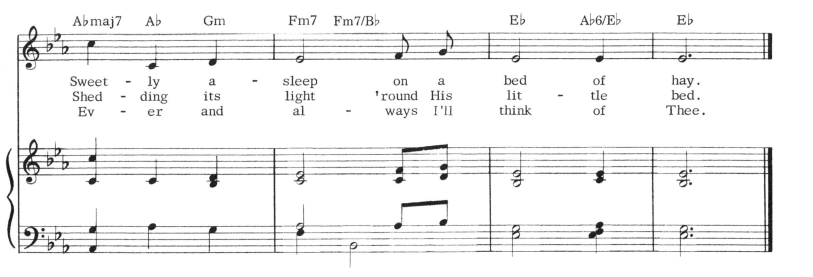

| A♭maj7 | A♭ | Gm | | Fm7 | Fm7/B♭ | | | E♭ | A♭6/E♭ | E♭ |

Sweet - ly a - sleep on a bed of hay.
Shed - ding its light 'round His lit - tle bed.
Ev - er and al - ways I'll think of Thee.

The Final Carol 1954: As Al faced his final days, he completed his last carol. He knew death was near. The carol was a prelude that Al knew; it was so simple in its musical character. Friday, the fifth day of February, he finished it. Jimmy Joyce played it for him, but our praises did not deter him from altering the tenor line in the last eight bars. Al was always sure of his musical harmonies.

His death came two days later in an ambulance en route to a hospital. Ironically, the signed contract from Columbia Records arrived by special messenger just an hour after his death. His mortal life had ended but his musical life would begin.

I chose this as the final card, signed just "Anne and Diane." It was the most elaborate we had ever sent, being printed by Columbia Records. The young child on the front page was the age of Diane when her father died. But the wonder and joy of Christmas was Al's gift to Diane throughout his illness. As with his parents, Al was able to overcome death, leaving a legacy of beauty, music, love, and faith to his family. What greater gift could a child ask of a father!

In April, 1954, the final recording of the first album, *The Christmas Mood*, was completed. In November, our Christmas card was given as a gift to the world. I wrote a note on the 1954 card, the cover a reprint of the album cover, to announce to the friends and family that the tradition was ending.

It was a sad moment for me as I realized the loss of a friend, husband, father of my daughter, Diane, and the musical spirit that was Alfred Burt. Only my last promise to Al, to care for his music and his daughter, shaped my future. I stumbled, I suffered, but as the years passed, my goal to see that Al's music survived gave me the impetus to live. Now I know God's plan was greater than my needs. The joy, inspiration, and beauty of the Burt Carols is our musical legacy of love, now shared at the happiest of all seasons, Christmas. Al so wanted to have his music appreciated. As we have watched its growth, Diane and I are proud and happy to share our Christmas cards with you, the world family. May you and your family enjoy a very musical Christmas and God's fullest blessings in the year ahead.

Anne S. Burt

DISCOGRAPHY

AH, BLEAK AND CHILL THE WINT'RY WIND (1,2,4)
Singers Unlimited *Christmas* – Polygram

ALL ON A CHRISTMAS MORNING (1,2,4)
John Williams/Boston Pops/Tanglewood Festival Chorus *We Wish You A Merry Christmas* – Polygram

BRIGHT, BRIGHT THE HOLLY BERRIES (see This Is Christmas)

CAROL OF THE MOTHER (Sleep Baby Mine) (2,4)
George Winston *December: 20th Anniversary Edition* – RCA Victor

CAROLING, CAROLING (1,2,3,4)
John Williams/Boston Pops/Tanglewood Festival Chorus *We Wish You A Merry Christmas* – Polygram
Ralph Carmichael *Big Band Christmas* – Intersound
Nat King Cole *The Christmas Song* – Capitol
Natalie Cole *Holly And Ivy* – Elektra
First Call *The Alfred Burt Christmas Carols Golden Anniversary Collection* – VAG (distributor: Collegium 800-367-9059)
The King Family *The Alfred Burt Christmas Carols Golden Anniversary Collection* – VAG (distributor: Collegium 800-367-9059)
Maureen McGovern *The Alfred Burt Christmas Carols Golden Anniversary Collection* – VAG (distributor: Collegium 800-367-9059)
Manhattan Transfer *The Christmas Album* – Sony
Johnny Mathis *Christmas Eve With Johnny Mathis* – Sony
Singers Unlimited *Christmas* – Polygram
Fred Waring & The Pennsylvanians *Caroling, Caroling* – EMI Special Products

CHRIST IN THE STRANGER'S GUISE (1,2,4)
John Williams/Boston Pops/Tanglewood Festival Chorus *We Wish You A Merry Christmas* – Polygram

CHRISTMAS COMETH CAROLING (2,4)
George Winston *The Alfred Burt Christmas Carols Golden Anniversary Collection* – VAG (distributor: Collegium 800-367-9059)

COME, DEAR CHILDREN (1,2,3,4)
John Williams/Boston Pops/Tanglewood Festival Chorus *We Wish You A Merry Christmas* – Polygram
Lex De Azevedo with Millennium Choir *The Alfred Burt Christmas Carols Golden Anniversary Collection* – VAG (distributor: Collegium 800-367-9059)

JESU PARVULE (1,2,3,4)
John Williams/Boston Pops/Tanglewood Festival Chorus *Joy To The World* – Sony
Singers Unlimited *Christmas* – Polygram

NIGH BETHLEHEM (1,2,4)
John Williams/Boston Pops/Tanglewood Festival Chorus *Joy To The World* – Sony
Singers Unlimited *Christmas* – Polygram

O HEARKEN YE (1,2,3,4)
John Williams/Boston Pops/Tanglewood Festival Chorus *We Wish You A Merry Christmas* – Polygram
Lex De Azevedo with Millennium Choir *The Alfred Burt Christmas Carols Golden Anniversary Collection* – VAG (distributor: Collegium 800-367-9059)
Tennessee Ernie Ford *The Alfred Burt Christmas Carols Golden Anniversary Collection* – VAG (distributor: Collegium 800-367-9059)
Fred Waring & The Pennsylvanians *The Alfred Burt Christmas Carols Golden Anniversary Collection* – VAG (distributor: Collegium 800-367-9059)

SOME CHILDREN SEE HIM (1,2,3,4)
John Williams/Boston Pops/Tanglewood Festival Chorus *We Wish You A Merry Christmas* – Polygram
Perry Como *The Greatest Christmas Songs* – RCA
Bing Crosby & Mary Martin *Bing Celebrates Christmas With Family & Friends* – DVD
Tennessee Ernie Ford & The Roger Wagner Chorale *The Story Of Christmas* – Capitol
Dave Grusin *The Alfred Burt Christmas Carols Golden Anniversary Collection* – VAG (distributor: Collegium 800-367-9059)
Al Jarreau *Christmas* – Rhino
Nancy LaMott *Just In Time For Christmas* – MID
Kenny Loggins *December* – Sony
Mannheim Steamroller *Christmas Extraordinaire* – American Gramophone
James Taylor *At Christmas* – Columbia
Andy Williams *The Alfred Burt Christmas Carols Golden Anniversary Collection* – VAG (distributor: Collegium 800-367-9059)
George Winston *December: 20th Anniversary Edition* – RCA Victor

THE STAR CAROL (1,2,4)
John Williams/Boston Pops/Tanglewood Festival Chorus *Joy To The World* – Sony
The Hi-Lo's *This Time It's Love* – Collectables
Peggy Lee *Christmas With Peggy Lee* – Capitol
Aaron Neville *Best of Aaron Neville/ The Christmas Collection* – A & M
Simon & Garfunkel *Old Friends; Dreaming Of A White Christmas* – Sony

THIS IS CHRISTMAS (Bright, Bright The Holly Berries) (1,2,3,4)
Julie Andrews *The Alfred Burt Christmas Carols Golden Anniversary Collection* – VAG (distributor: Collegium 800-367-9059)
John Williams/Boston Pops/Tanglewood Festival Chorus *Joy To The World* – Sony
Singers Unlimited *Christmas* – Polygram

WE'LL DRESS THE HOUSE (1,2,3,4)
John Williams/Boston Pops/Tanglewood Festival Chorus *Joy To The World* – Sony
Lex De Azevedo with Millennium Choir *The Alfred Burt Christmas Carols Golden Anniversary Collection* – VAG (distributor: Collegium 800-367-9059)

WHAT ARE THE SIGNS (2,4)
Singers Unlimited *Christmas* – Polygram
George Winston *The Alfred Burt Christmas Carols Golden Anniversary Collection* – VAG (distributor: Collegium 800-367-9059)

ALBUM (1)
Columbia Choir and Ralph Carmichael Brass Ensemble *The Christmas Mood* – VAG (distributor: Collegium 800-367-9059)

ALBUM (2)
The Voices of Jimmy Joyce *This Is Christmas* – VAG (distributor: Collegium 800-367-9059)

ALBUM (3)
The Caroling Company *A Christmas Present* – VAG (distributor: Collegium 800-367-9059)

ALBUM (4)
Springbrook Singers *Inland Northwest Christmas* – Orchard